How the Light is Spent

To Kati,
Amazing!
Thank you so much,
Gail Sidonie Sobat

How the Light is Spent

by

Gail Sidonie Sobat

WINTERGREEN
STUDIOS PRESS

Wintergreen Studios Press
P.O. Box 75, Yarker, ON, Canada K0K 3N0

Book design and front cover design by Rena Upitis
Back cover photo by Geoff McMaster
Edited by Bruce Kauffman
Composed in Book Antiqua and Candara, typefaces designed by Monotype Typography and Gary Munch, respectively

Library and Archives Canada Cataloguing in Publication
Sobat, Gail Sidonie

How the Light is Spent/Gail Sidonie Sobat

ISBN-10: 0986547395 EAN-13: 978-0-9865473-9-3
1. Poetry — Canadian.

I.   Title. How the Light is Spent

Legal Deposit – Library and Archives Canada

Other books by Gail Sidonie Sobat

Ingamald (2001)

Aortic Caprice (2003/2004)

A Winter's Tale (2004)

The Book of Mary (2006)

A Glass Darkly (2006)

Gravity Journal (2008)

Chance to Dance for You (2011)

In the Graveyard (2011)

Not With a Bang (2012)

For Jeannie and Tat, TLF

Table of Contents

Badlands 1

Bohunks from the Hills...3

Storylines 5

Mine Yours 7

Coal mad..8

short pants 9

From Rosedale to Cambria Suite..............................10

Outside the Mine Store...14

Jeannie Gets a Job at Clare's....................................17

Nice Legs 20

Main Street Drumheller...22

in the mine...23

Abandon January 24

surrender 25

Journal, February 12, 1940..26

in and out like a lion 27

Crazy in 1943...28

Remembrance Day 29

Missing in Action 30

Patri 32

my mother's hands...33

'when the bough breaks' 34

red sweater 35

From the valley 38

P/O   M. E. VanDeKinder..39

couldn't...42

Drumheller Graveyard...43

Sailing to Byzantium 45

sailing to Byzantium...47

bottle blonde on the golden horn 48

Saturday in Etiler 49

On the Way to the Grand Bazaar.................................50

Istanbul #1...51

Istanbul #2...52

the day they closed Istanbul down..............................55

contractions...56

where at last is home? 57

reading through the travel journal..............................59

pagan..60

come home to find 61

brevity..62

How the Light is Spent.. 63

vertigo..65

meditations from a less than athlete 66

Lessons from the Greeks..67

Equinox Circumvenio 68

Snow is promised...69

In November..70

February snowfall 71

stilllife winter..72

when I consider how my light is spent 73

lunatic plunges to near death while delivering trash to the

alley 74

why do birds insistent sing at four a.m.? 75

Urban crow 76

world woes 78

Du bist die Ruh 79

Breakdown on the Merritt Highway 81

Fecal Incident on the Sunshine Coast 82

sea sojourn 83

no Milton, maybe D. H. Lawrence 84

eye spider 86

pilgrimage to Hardware Grill 88

Tipscoggling 92

marking time 94

Acknowledgements 97

Badlands

Bohunks from the Hills

your family
hails from the badlands
those that once coughed up
black sputum
to fuel the machinations of the rich
your grandfather
swung across the Red Deer River
where your mother aunts cousins
all swam

your mother lived in a shack
where night mice
skittered the walls
disappointed the crumbs
were so few
still her mother fed the hobos
desperate men who rode the rails
hats in hands
accepted her bohunk food

this is your valley, too
though its red shale depresses you
ghosts of what was who were unsettle
dust from the hills

these badlands are lonely lands
despite childhood joys
misplaced memories
these hills hold neither charm nor hope
remind instead that loss
is so sadly permanent

while histories stories loves lives
wear down wash away
surely as the silt from these bad hills

.

Storylines

admire the line of her arms
in the sunlight
she is hanging clothes
along the prairie clothesline
cursing the wind that catches them up
hoists them into the April mud

admire the way she lights a cigarette
traces her lips with red desire
pulls on her stockings
mindbends her hair
paints on eyebrows

admire her teeth in a glass
hair in perm curlers
cutting and trimming
corns and calluses

she has the laughter
of a flirtatious seventeen-year-old
although she is pushing eighty
laughter spilling freely
like wine from a glass

she is old
older than you'd like her to be
older than she'd ever dreamed possible
more obstinate
forgetful
the world and her stepping through it
pains her

admire her path
it is not what you would choose
but oh the stories
once twice many times told
oh the stories

Mine Yours

you say I'll never know
what you meant to each other
that long ago once upon life
when you loved a boyman
who loved you for all
your smalltown hillside ways
the flip of your light brown hair
his quick brief smile
shaped your life to come to this
so tell me
let me mine your stories

Coal mad

coal is a thick vein through this valley
black as the owners' hearts
the same who send men for pennies
down into ill-lit tombs
drilling and dynamiting
hoping the beams will hold
coal gas won't poison
lungs won't blacken
'god knows the bastards have it good
only communists want unions'
coal seeps into pores, the mind
sullies a man's outlook
steals the daylight and substitutes
a black vitriolic madness

short pants

saw you
with your crooked grin
too-short pants
leaning against the lamp post
looking

heard you
laughing with the guys
trying too hard
horseplaying on the corner
when I walked by

watched you
help your stern-faced mother
washing windows
turn your face from their shine
to mine

then at the dance
your hand on the small of my back
caught my heart by surprise

From Rosedale to Cambria Suite

I
this valley is old
this village Cambria
where trilobites flourished
in a great sea
yet my people and yours
come from the old country
to a land
so new it does not admit easily
those with names that trip the tongue

II
we will change our names
forsake our mother tongue
adopt the new and forget the old
see if we can forge a life
beneath these scarred hills
where seams of black
determine our fate
half a year's work or
half a year's relief
doesn't matter when
you owe your life to the mine

III
black-faced the men
take the swinging bridge
across the river
you wash your father's back

careful to avoid the mole
that disgusts you
a silence fills the shack
your mother and father are fighting
tonight after borscht and heavy bread
pyrohy and holobtsi
he will storm out to the other woman
and you will run under the stars
towards the boy with too-short pants
who understands you are trapped
as a canary

IV
one room school is good enough
for the likes of all of you
with funny sounding names
funny smells from your houses and mouths
learn the king's English
learn the history of the Dominion and the Empire
learn above all your place
go to school barefoot and grateful

V
neither toy nor book in the shack that is home
outhouse and Sears catalogue
water pump near the cow and chickens
homework by the oil lamp on the rough table
only a crackling old radio brings
the world to this dry-boned depressed valley
you share your bed with your older sibling
watch the mice skitter up the sides of the walls
draw the covers over your head
fear small rodents all your life

VI
once you had a doll
rough sewn body with porcelain face
nowhere your own to place her
she sat atop the door jam
until the slamming shook and toppled her
so many broken pieces swept up by your ailing mother
.

VII
never went hungry
not for food
your mother slaughtered and plucked
kneaded and baked
scalded and boiled
churned and churned
gathered and sorted
washed and rolled
carried and swept
scrimped and saved
so that no one went dirty
no one went hungry
not even the hobos who saw the sign:
"kind-hearted woman lives here"
some railrider carved into the fencepost

VIII
your mother's heart burst at last
worn out from trying to live
you the youngest child of too many
have nothing left in the dale of roses

but an elder brother
a bitter sister
an indifferent father
and your own cracked heart

IX
when your mother dies and you are ten
your father marries the other woman
the widow with five kids of her own
and no other room in her heart
the tastes of food change
her nachynka is blander
studenetz are runnier

suddenly though you are ten
you are grown up
with growing concerns
your father wants you out
one less mouth to feed
small wonder you fall
in love with a blue-eyed boy
when you are but thirteen

you'll be lucky if you make it to grade 9
so you are happy to reach grade 11
until he throws you out
and you get a job at the dress shop
$8.00 a week
where the Jewish owners are kindly
don't mind that you are a Ukrainian girl
from Rosedale village

Outside the Mine Store

Hey Mar-cellll…
hey Tat is that
what they call you?
kinda like you
I mean
kinda like it
when you
come by
hang out
nice blue eyes
you got Tat
from your dad
call me Jeannie
call on me
sometime
ride your bike
on over
to Rosedale
would ya
sometime
Marcel
I mean
Tat?

Jeannie Gets a Job at Clare's

that suit's wool gabardine
there's worsted jerseys and crepes
these dresses are cheaper cotton muslin

$3.95 a piece
this is a seersucker jacket
that's velvet and taffeta
for the fancy customers
like the mayor's plump wife

this one's got a peplum
just like Joan Crawford wears
houndstooth herringbone tweeds
paisley calico gingham prints
camelhair angora lambs wool
cable knit cardigan cashmere
in mood indigo Kelly green or chartreuse
midnight black is hard to match

$7.95 for an
a-line empire or drop waist
with a sweetheart cowl or boat neck
batwing bell sleeves cap or cape
straight skirt swing gored or slitted
swing jackets and tailored sports
for those specially daring
these Kate Hepburn trousers

merchandise and spin around
measure the waist the bust
the arms the hips the legs
alterations affectations
wait on the customers
for the paycheque or closing
on murderous high heels
pumps mules or open toe slings

there she is
the one from the village
that beautiful girl
pinning up a hem
tucking in a pleat
dressing up the window
looks a little like Hayworth
waiting to be discovered

Nice Legs

nice legs
you always told me you had
in the photos
you lift your skirt
in the Red Deer River
pose à la Grable
at the public swimming pool
million dollars insurance
for Betty's in Hollywood
not yours from the bohunk shack

at secretarial college
you struggled through shorthand
@ seventeen &
learned to type
ω widowed hands
on the underwood keys
jjj kkk lll sss
until you could accurately
make 60 words a minute
100 could get you 5¢ more/hour
especially in triplicate
& if you had nice legs

Main Street Drumheller

there's a dance at the Elk's tonight
Friday night and the boys on leave will be there
so will you in your fuchsia jersey
the new one from the store where you work
just got a ten cent raise so splurged
on this dream of a dress that drapes and caresses
swings when you walk or foxtrot or jitterbug

the band is local and pretty damn hot
your cousin slipped you a little gin and orange
so your beautiful legs feel firecrackers
when "In the Mood" begins   someone leads you
to the dance floor and another waits
for "Rum and Coca Cola"
still another for "Satin Doll"

outside the streets are dancing too
this smalltown that will one day ghost
is hopping and laughing loud
the corner café is full to capacity
but you squeeze into a booth together
young and unaware of the war
all promise before your valley eyes

elsewhere there are cities bigger
nightclubs flash smart doormen greet
women drip with furs and jewels
the band is better paid and famous
shopgirls like you dream of more
but here tonight   this dry town
may as well be Chicago

in the mine

in the mine a man
loses his soul you said
unlike your Belgian-born father before you
you couldn't commit yourself
to that grave
would no longer play the canary
to Star Mine Inc.

so you signed those recruitment papers
lied about your age
they pretending to believe
          who would take that boyish grin for eighteen
took you
faster than you could think
change your mind
or mine

Abandon January

here in blue cold January
toes and fingers numb
still my heart blazes
despite the rigidity of the season
passion flows well enough in my veins
reminding me that Florence would be fine
for lovers such as we

except that we are only
two cold prairie lovers too poor
for anything but fancy
the only exotic climate that between us

so if I put
pomegranate lips persuasively
upon your mouth, your stomach
your Michelangelo thighs

in the morning will we rise
abashedly or boldly
will we love again
will we return
to this blue cold January
numb but warmed by
making at long last love

surrender

a kiss
abandon
will
power
is there ecstasy in dying?

Journal, February 12, 1940

in the morning
if you but glance
at the blue sky
pristine snow
hieroglyphics writ on frosted panes
you can believe for a moment
the world does not march to war

in and out like a lion

the hills are brown and somber
birds chirrup half-heartedly
as a wind whips across the sear grass
hands chafe at March's cold reminder
of a killing climate

Crazy in 1943

we marry against
all better judgment
my sister won't talk to me
your parents too poor
to make it to Calgary
a friend stands up for us

the doctor won't sign
already lost a son
girls who are married
then widowed
are damaged goods
dented cans

they all say

we're crazy
in love
so we do

Remembrance Day

remember
the last leave before you went overseas
you took my nylon stockings
the best I had
ones without runs
tied my hands to the hotel bedstead

we ran fast that afternoon
faster than my stockings

I took them to the mender
but he said it was hopeless
left them with him anyway
just in case — I still had hope
but after the telegram
I never bothered to pick them up

Missing in Action

the telegram came
I fell to my knees
my sister says
I don't remember any of it
something bone china
in me cracked
like the set you sent me for Christmas
from England
now I can no longer pour hot tea
into that translucent cup

STOP

I bought dresses
went to dances
wept nights empty
watched day dawn
dashed to the dress shop
half-believed another telegram
would one day arrive

STOP

Previous telegram mistake
STOP
Private Marcel injured but alive
STOP
Discovered disoriented but well
Returning May 1944
STOP
Sends his love

STOP

No such message ever arrives
I carry on this smalltown existence
shopping selling
eating dancing
weeping grieving
living

STOP

Patri

on the last day of my grade eleven year
before my father kicked me out
forced me to go to work at fifteen
Miss Hayes taught us the poem
"Dulce et Decorum est"

I found the Latin hard for my tongue
though it had lost its Ukrainian cadence
Latin was for mass and I was lapsed
but in 1941 the meaning was clear enough
and I didn't believe the lie of glory

not then or in '43 when you
survived but twenty minutes of battle
as navigator until your plane and crew
without pomp or ceremony
were spewed over a foreign country

he said I was a burden
another mouth to feed
too much for my stepmother to handle
so I packed that tightly in my bags
headed into town resenting the lies of our fathers

my mother's hands

my mother's hands
soft and careworn
blue-veined speak
of dishes dreams
broken or forgotten

where once
they anxiously
inquired after temperatures
fumbled for cigarettes
teased hair to a tizzy
plucked brows to extinction
fussed over diapers dinners
now they deal cards
in solitude for solitaire
calm repetition

on my mother's hands
writ on crepe-paper skin
are liver spots
of poverty
orphanhood at ten
widowhood at seventeen
motherhood too early too late
an unspoken lifetime

my mother's hands
wisely certain
accepting no argument
urge me onward away

'when the bough breaks'

the eyes of my wise grandmother
recall the death of a favourite son
embattled but twenty minutes
until bits of his body flew all over England

her eyes see a grave she never saw
one of a field of white crosses
undistinguished
like his brief career in the forces

they send our children off to die
so children die
and mothers with arms bereft
can only rock themselves

red sweater

I don my red shoes
        just because they're sensible
        doesn't mean they have to be boring
and I cross 97th Street
where I live
        where they put old people like me
        too poor to pay for better
I cross 97th Street
and head for the A&N
        that's Army and Navy to you

my daughter
        from far away in Toronto land
        out of guilt or remorse for
        some ugly thing said
        in some telephone conversation
sent me fifty dollars
and I've had my eye on a new toaster
        nothing like toast and jam
        of a cold winter afternoon
        and winter's coming sure as death

so I whoosh through those doors
        no one holds a door for you these days
the moment they open
go down in the basement where the bargains are
        damn these old knees
and I find a Sunbeam
        now there's a make
        you don't often see anymore
        probably swallowed up
        by some giant company

       and all the parts made in Japan
carry my prize up the arthritic ascend

that's when I spy them
on a homely display table
cashmere sweaters
       soft as those blankets Tat and I tumbled into
       that long ago sunny summer day
       when he promised he would always love me
       and I believed it and he did too
       only we didn't know the war
       would kill the bridegroom
       and I'd singly raise a single daughter
       next door to shame, my only neighbour

I draw my liver-spotted hand through soft woolens
like a lover along the face of the beloved
set that toaster down for a spell
look at the knit
       very fine
check the seams
       I've been taken before
where it's made
       good old England
       where Tat lies or what's left of him
rub the sweater against my face
not too near my lipstick
       yes, I still wear it
       I'm not quite dead
       and I think the bright shades go best
       now that my hair's white
glance at the price
and all the colours
butter cream yellow

ripe plum, deep sea navy
tea rose, caramel candy

then I spy it
red delicious candy apple
       my favourite colour
       like my shoes
last one left
hold my breath
look at the size
small
       like me
I just leave that toaster sitting there

this autumn afternoon
I'll sit down to tea and CBC
in my favourite chair near the window
in my old apartment
look out at the rummies and druggies
try to feel safe
think I'll leave these red shoes on
touch up my lipstick
put my feet up on the furniture
maybe pour a little of that last bit of sherry
who needs toast
when you've got a bright red sweater

From the valley

you can smell the coal dust
some say it smells of money
others of early death
mothers warn the children to avoid
any oxidizing masses
red shale quicksand to sinkholes
where the black brute seething
beneath can burn and maim

these weather-beaten hills mark a life
of human scars and disappointment
but when the meadowlark sings at dawn
with the sky alight in pink and salmon
against the crevices and hoodoos
that coal dust scent recalls
Depression and wartime and you
a simple girl from Rosedale come home

P/O M. E. VanDeKinder

you were always a picture
a handsome boyish face
with my grandfather's eyes and smile
the father I never had but wanted

flipping through photos
returned late in life to the girl
whose brown hair is white
how could she not love you?

there you are in the Hyde Park
'seem happy, sweet, but
pretty lonely and sad that day'
mere days from death

photos of her barely seventeen
full of Drumheller dreams
naïve unaware in beauty
all that loss yet to come

well-meaning family
gave her your military cap
today on our visit
wrapped in wilted tissue

she took its wool peak in hand
raised it to her lips
how strange to be the daughter
watching the mother

there are no happy endings
just the brief joys of living
and if lucky, loving
a boy from the hills even once

couldn't

back when I was seventeen
and you not eighteen
couldn't wait
in 1943
for the war to end
couldn't wait
to feel your chest
heart fluttering against mine
couldn't wait
for cooler heads
there was no cooling
that summer of 1943
couldn't wait
to cover each other
trace our beautiful bodies
kiss away fear and regret
couldn't wait
to marry before a justice of the peace
then march off to war
meet that bigamist death
who wouldn't

Drumheller Graveyard

you clean up the graves
among the sear grass
the headstones have shifted
or worse fallen from
time the great leveler

your city-raised daughter
does not even remember
the names of these
only vaguely recalling faces
from photos faded forgotten

you too will end up in a drawer
no one will know your name
was Genya or Jeannie not Jean
all of a solitary life returned
to valley dust and coal ash

does no one care for the dead
you wonder wandering
among these derelict graves
over by the east wall
the grass is greener

your thoughts are sober
later over beer at the Elks
at tables sit old people
you almost remember
are old yourself

tomorrow the drive home
will be long and quiet
anxious to leave this sad valley
these hills in the background
such a relief

Sailing to Byzantium

sailing to Byzantium

I am sailing to Byzantium
the hardest journey
this mariner has ever made

no exotic perfumes
will match your eastern spice
erase your quixotic quietude

will ever fingers mine
stroke India ink hair
thick as night, fragrant as curry
like yours again

will agate eyes like yours
gaze across the Bosphorus
and then into mine
tempting abandon

will I hear your honey voice
in tones the muezzin
chant in Asian waves
upon my ears

and what will I put in place of
my heart
cut out by your albatross beak

bottle blonde on the golden horn

here in another world
I am alien
Camus' stranger
I do not like the sour smell of the people
their glares hostile accusatory
I am a wicked beacon
of the American way
embodiment of evil

I have been swindled by gypsies
shoe shine boys
duplicitous children rob
me of lira
my sense of assurance
their grimy fingers
pluck my most vulnerable chords

I see the bridge and the minaret
against a filthy dawn sky
cough up yesterday's dirt and grime
wonder if there is anything
clean and pure to be found
in this Janus-faced city

Saturday in Etiler

on a grey Istanbul day
a mist settles over everything
even the gypsies, their colours, their horses
seem muted and sluggish
the Bosphorus is muddied
with the effluents of millions
the sun is a dullard
who will not show his face for shame
birds fly listlessly
the muezzin's call to prayer
fogs the brain
people in this land do not know who they are
and the weather tells them so

On the Way to the Grand Bazaar

our taxi coils through streets impossibly narrow
the driver speaks of socialism
but his cab coughs us out in the midst of garrulous
                                        barterers
screaming for our attention
eyeing our clothes our queer ways

a famished peasant woman clutches the sleeve of a
                                        passerby
shakes a fist at his indifference
a devout unfurls his multi-coloured carpet
at midday call to prayer
so we all know which direction is east

a cripple dances for lira on his stumps for legs
a maimed child pulls herself along the ground
skinny street cats
tortoise, black, calico
thread between our legs

a blind man plays an ancient air
on a time-beaten ney at the street corner
where a gypsy holds forth her bandaged child
to move our hearts to pity
our hands to our purses

and observing it all in the background
the Aya Sofya
smiling benignly

Istanbul #1

I miss your ways
when you come gentle
into my good morn
when I for lack of laughter
find a well of mirth in you
I miss the understood
and the understated
your critic's eye
and pointed wit

now
the windows of the world are
awash with weary
and the songs all sound the same

now
I drag my feet upon the stair
one click of key in lock
admits me to the stale air

of missing

Istanbul #2

in and out of dreams
falsity and whimsy
take you to the imaginary
trust me...I'm telling you lies

go to the land of sultans
taste food of strange spice
dance to music and song
ears tuned to a foreign key
drink in the call to prayer
turn yourself to the east in wonder
five times daily
always on the edge of this and some other time

see the women
swathed in black
whose eyes accuse, accept, acquiesce
or those who mimic the harlotry of the west
women discerned always and only
through thick and noxious cigarette smoke
through the eyes of men and Allah
always always upon you

taste cinnamon
bitter and pungent mixed with mint and meat
dumplings swimming in yogurt
fresher than today
quaff virulent raki
until you waken with licorice-clouded eyes
to tramp another day through the medieval city
to the Golden Horn

to touch the woven fibers
made by women sold by men
in the centuries-old bazaar
sip hospitable teas
with barterers smiling benignly through tooth-rot
wind labyrinthine and lost
through ancient alleys of ancient barters
deceit and treachery, death some say

fish the Bosphorus
or worse swim in her putrid waters
deceptively blue and calm
feel the spray
of her angriest mood whip
across your western face
sail her glass surface
in the sun, in the dark, under Islamic crescent moon

be dealt a sour hand by the gypsies
have your palm's silver palmed
be swept up in national fervour and weep the
anthem or soccer rally or Ottoman victory cry
laze sleepily on the dock
with the hungry street cats
the hungry street-wise urchins
await the daily catch from the rough, sea-weary fishers

wonder if you'll live through another day
or see another night
exhausted by the toxic fumes of
stinking auto breath
die from heat or loneliness
ignorance or ideology
yours or theirs
in Istanbul the mix is poison as the scorpion's sting

the day they closed Istanbul down

there was silence
peace at last in the streets
for one single day
the fundamentalists and secularists
got along
Muslim, Christian, and Jew
co-existed harmoniously
the poor and the rich
stayed inside
played with their kids
sang songs
smoked quiet cigarettes
the yelling and the screaming
of human and machine voice
stopped suddenly at dawn
you could hear the birds
smell the salt in the Bosphorus spray
believe for one short day
until the setting of the sun
that anything
even in the most unlikely, unexpected places
is possible

contractions

a clean slate
new life
new land
who would ever think
there'd be so much amniotic goo

where at last is home?

thought you knew
that place to unroll your sleeping bag
fill your ashtray with the buts of dreams
anesthetize before the god of flickering images
flickering spiritual mantras
you can buy a ring and a promise
from the slick star-aged demigod
lost as you are

in his arms or her arms or
tangled in a sea of arms and legs
if it feels good
must be love
must be home
must be

with friends
smiling and gay
lift the spirits and your glasses
laugh harder, hardest
'til you know
this is as good as it gets
good as it gets

nearer to nature
find your totem
beat the drum
collect all the shells
rocks and pine cones
you can because baby
the elements will kill you

if they can if you're stupid enough
to fall asleep too near the water's
or the cliff's or the heart's edge

amidst the family
those damned smiling villains
beaming benignly from pages
of familial photo albums
bound with failure and filial obligation

where the hat is hung
and are all the boxes stuffed with loss
boxes stuffed with all we cannot part withal
stuffed into corners, under beds, in skeletal closets
for someday's instant recall
lest we forget who we are
who we were

here where we are still
and the moment blurs
past and present into nanosecond
and future has no place in thoughts
of mortality
cannot see the horizon
cannot see for weeping
for home
are you?

reading through the travel journal

runaway come home again
colours of Istanbul   chalk paintings in the rain
remember the moon on the Bosphorus
grilled meat on the breeze
whirling dervish memories

retrace a sultan's footsteps
heart leap to the rhythm of ney and drum
stand on a rooftop terrace
while the sun sets golden behind the dome
women smile behind their veils

caress the bazaar-bought carpet
strain to hear the call to prayer
taste the sweetness of Turkish delight
wipe sugar powder from fingers
close them tight to fend off an evil eye

all fright and chagrin
mere travel whimsy
Constantinople construct
diluted by distance
time-tempered

a gypsy whispers through cracked yellow teeth
"what makes you think you could ever leave
what makes you think you were ever here"
a beggar claws at your purse of recall
when you check your pocket it's empty

pagan

pagan blood runs through these veins
a pulse tuned to distant drums
nasal songsters
dances with veils
an eye turned eastward, wayward
ever elsewhere

but I live in the suburbs
near a great mall
where children do not dance in the streets
neither gypsies nor tinkers
tender wares at my window
and no one is singing

still I light the incense and the candle
let a moony otherworld in through the curtain
tune my strings to a minor Asian scale
and play at pagan possibilities
boiling in the blood
roiling in a restless soul

come home to find

I think I am losing myself
and just in the nick of time
I was almost found
and then what?

no poet's angst
indefinable romantic longing
songs unsung
exhausting moonlight caprices
pulse untuned
neo-tragic heartstring requiems

what indeed would I do
if ever I found myself
at last
and anticlimactically
between a rock and a hard place

brevity

incense clouds the mind
billows the lungs
reminds you that
somewhere once
you lived far away
upon a time
where spice markets
are thousands of years old
bartering is the means
to make a living
a quick sale
a tidy profit
where minarets and cupolas
clutter the horizon
against a golden sunset
you are called to prayer
to remember
that you got through
tomorrow and tomorrow is another
that life is precious and rich
as the dark thick coffee
in the demitasse

How the Light is Spent

vertigo

geese call across
murky Alberta skies
summoning the faithful
for a southern return

I'd like to glide along
but have no sense of direction
fear of heights

October guns are pointed skyward
to cull the graceless
weakest or wing-damaged

what hope have I
with clay feet and heart
of reaching the vanishing point

meditations from a less than athlete

no poetry
but surely a poet in motion
stumbling through October

a last goose honks encouragement
but the callow leaves
laugh dryly derisive
at my awkward antics
though there is a smattering of applause
from an earnest birch
as I wheeze clumsily by

the sun is weak as my knees
but I take heart
between the shadows
and the spasms
that there is still a pulse
a graceless rhythm
in this fumble towards mortality

Lessons from the Greeks

I was a happy adolescent
when I learned
that in Greece
women can be gods
powerful with desires and demands
like any in the bombastic male pantheon

Achilles I know little about
except that he hurt his heel
or his mother did
when dipping him upsidedown in the River Styx
      a strawberry to chocolate
as would any sensible maternal goddess

Like him we limp towards mortality
let us hope though
as we reach our nether years
that no arrow likewise
pierces poisonous our heels

Instead let us, like Epicureus
eat, drink, be merry
find another use for Trojans
than making war

Equinox Circumvenio

the sparrows stop talking when you walk by
resume their loquacious mutterings only after you pass
similarly the leaves whisper behind your back
thought you heard the lilac bush laughing
the wind wheedling wisecracks

it seems love that
some fallen branch jealous of our green love
pointed us out in the arbour
that yellow day in the park under a cool blue sky
and told all the others

now the geese gossip overhead
spread rumour and innuendo southwards
you and a girl half your boy half her age
whip the moulting leaves to a frenzy of envy
for no one knows except us how best to cheat autumn

Snow is promised

snow coming they say
the sky still is streaked with blue hope
though the wind raises a cruel hand to the cheek

a heart tosses in the tempest like the spruce limbs
desire flutters to the ground with the other dead
                                        leaves
raise the eyes in case the clouds should fall

wish for another autumnal respite, however brief
snow on Sunday
not a dare but a promise

In November

in November
snow is ankle deep
squirrels slip into lethean dreams
a chill halo circles the moon
who has turned a cold shoulder

the backyard world
still in slumber
songbirds flitted southwards
now only the stalwart chickadees sing
punctuated by those overdressed magpies

birdfeeder needs filling
walks shoveling
doorsteps sweeping
throughout a colourless month
signifying death

belied only by this beating heart
and the scarlet mountain ash berries

February snowfall

icing sugar dusts the regal oak
soaring pines
stunted hedges
uncertain cedars

lone meandering squirrel
shakes the coating
from the branches
as he flits for food

a broadloom of white
trails the path to the bench
shrouds the birdbath
covers the step

all the walks will need sweeping
again today and tonight
perhaps tomorrow
and tomorrow

but for now this soft flurry
stills my hand at its work
slows my blood as though sap
stops my breath at the pane

stilllife winter

a ball of white fluff
jackrabbit dozing
on my frozen lawn
as the sun sleepily rises
through the chill winter day
I am stunned at nature's gift
given me this morning
huddled slumbering
safe from city coyote
to be admired from my window
as I sip my coffee
for a moment looking in on Eden

when I consider how my light is spent

the light is pink and blue
against the frost
birds do not give voice
to this chill morning
the puppy fogs the air
with eager breath
pulls at his leash
racing headlong into the day
but the light catches in my throat
and I resist his urging

lunatic plunges to near death while delivering trash to the alley

last night the lunar eclipse tricked me
in the dark my foot stumbled
between the house and alley
detritus of a life half lived
spilled across the snow
scrambling vainly to contain it all
I tumbled through shadow
landed unceremoniously
Lucifer fallen amidst
all the used or soiled or rejected
I looked upwards then as fools do
towards the light of lunacy

why do birds insistent sing at four a.m.?

the eastern sky still dark
like clockwork the warblers rise
call to prayer
call and response
rousing us from warm dream
fitful slumber
deepest somnolent peace
signal the insomniacs
anxious clock-watchers
it's bird time
to give up regret
hope of restful sleep
wasteful fretting
the birds are singing
day will dawn
morning will break
like the yellow yolk of a soft-boiled egg

Urban crow

urban crow you are
so much more gentrified
than your provincial cousins
those born of barns and backwoods
with their back country caws
crude crow vernacular

urbanely slick and sleekly black
preened for the downtown core
where competition may be stiff
demand exceeds supply
but pickings for the clever, canny, quick
can be raucously profitable

no windflight whimsies
or lazing somnolent in the sun
atop a farmer's fencepost
or stopping by for a casual chaw
at the ear of the strawman
in the parochial cornfield

the mind of an urban crow
is full of urgencies
a living to be made
negotiations to navigate
meetings on the roof of city hall
can be murder

amidst a crowing cacophony
all the hustle and bustle
of crow commerce

is a grave struggle
to stay aloft
in this survival of the fittest business

world woes

in Darfur the children cry
here gulls peck at a dry piece of discarded
life for the worldweary dreary

when a homeless man hands out the *Inner City Daily*
you know it's not good
news for the mired millennium

this neighbourhood does not tolerate prostitution
or so say the signs
lying all along 118th Street

a baby cries in a stairwell
two more freeze in their cold
poverty no match for the human dispirit

crow above the corpse of a girl
blood trailing to her peers
screams bloody murder

tonight this frost-gripped city
seems far from world woes
those so close as to touch

Du bist die Ruh

they said she was dying
could I sing in German?

in the room
the great empty shell of who she was
a farmer's wife

two thick hands
on the hospital blanket
once upon a memory
found the cow's teats
folded the thick pastry
soothed the sixth child's feverish brow
clutched the huge back of her man
threw dirt on his grave before her

I held the one good one still feeling
Du bist die Ruh, der Friede mild
softly not wishing to rouse

through the refrain did she
see again the misted morning cornfield
the trickling fickle brook
a vee of geese flying to or fro
faithful dog herding sheep to submission
clouds breezing across a harvest moon
logs blazing in the hearth
her mother's lined face

barely imperceptibly

Du bist die Ruh, der Friede mild
her hand squeezed mine

another lifetime ago
hearing Schubert
in another country
a young girl married a young boy
trusted a dream and a promise
left the fondly familiar
what became of that young life
spent here in this hospital bed

I sat imagining
singing this illusory truth:

Du bist die Ruh, der Friede mild

Du bist die Ruh, der Friede mild

Breakdown on the Merritt Highway

a sun so hot
sun so hot
you want to lizard-crawl beneath some rock
scorpion-scuttle into some crevice
when a car breakdown
reminds you of your mortality
in but a few
scorched breath-sucking minutes
when suddenly you wish
you'd brought that damned hat
even if it is ugly
realize that you drank
the last of the water an hour ago
squint along a swimming horizon
barren of civilization

remember all the Hollywood desert movies you've seen
even *Ishtar*
scouring their frames for survival tips
glance over at the panting dog of privilege
the dog you may have to kill
to drink its blood

then merciful angel of heaven
the semi engine of deus ex machina
with playboy bunny mudflaps
appears on the shimmering highway rise
gains on you slowly
hisses and farts to a blessed blessed stop

Fecal Incident on the Sunshine Coast

the dog took a dump in the Pacific
as we horrified mortified watched
even the seagull flapped off in disgust
no one thought to bring a bag
so off and outwards floated
two turds in the tide

wonder if they'll reach Japan
before disintegrating into nitrogen nothingness
if some coastal snorkler will
have a sudden scatological encounter
or might they circumnavigate the globe ocean by ocean
come back to us worldly wiser if lesser

maybe a revolted Pacific
too full of the effluents of billions
will simply toss them back ashore tomorrow
throwing in our faces the feces
a turgid turdish admonishment
to clean up our shit

sea sojourn

crickets call capriciously in the late afternoon
strains from a guitar sough across the sea breeze
the sun beams benignly from up high
along the sand a frothing panting canine frolic
one lone sailboat cavorts with the wind
you the solitary city dweller watch it all
cup in hand wishing only for a teaspoon of sugar
and another hundred years

no Milton, maybe D. H. Lawrence

when I consider how my light is spent
take a sip of coffee
stare out the window
a dog yipping somewhere
purr of heat register coming to life
a man asleep in the other room
disheveled under my covers
bone-tired after a night of me
my too-fat thighs
wrapped around his admiration
the world is an imperfect place

when I consider how my light is spent
leaf through seared pages
arthritic days wend to myopic years
my teeth grind down
my eyes turn grey
for kicks I take a turn or two
around the park looking for love empty bottles
whichever I find first
both are in such short supply these days
so I look to romance novels and young boys
alas the world is neither novel nor buoyant

I've considered the light before you know
I think it was a forty watt
dim enough for truth
to skulk in the shadows
that way I always look best
by candlelight and starlight
lately I've taken to shrouding the mirror

sporting dark shades drawing the blinds
next I think I'll wear the veil
handmaiden of Yahweh or Allah
or any of the succubi of this garish world

when I consider that my light is spent
getting and spending forking and doling
spreading and laying I am discomfited
to say the least which is the least I can say
o' for a muse of fire and all that crap
doesn't fit the bill in this sententious century
the world is full of ugly shriveled souls
jaundiced and vein-riddled parsimony
bloated paunches and bony fingers
clutching at pursestrings and undergarments
fools and poor players in a danse macabre

when I consider how my light is spent
out of step with this minuet
it gives me pause to peer out the window
there green and there blue
movement and leaf-stirrings
the dog has taken to yowling
my coffee cup needs refilling
a warmth between my legs prompts me
to wake the man in the next room
inspire him and conspire with him
how best to spend my light

eye spider

a spider lives inside my car
world within world within
webweaving eternal optimist
nothing six-legged to prey upon in here
and I'm much too big
to fall into her trap

still I pause in admiration
at the traffic light
such diligence and industry
hard to ignore
her web truly orb-catching
in the late madrush light

cannot bear to destroy the thing
or its maker
stowaway from a coastal sojourn
there spiders thrive in forests greenly deep
and unawares, passersby like me
can catch a falling arachnid in ferns a-tangle

sometimes I creep out beneath the northern lights
flashlight in hand to catch
a glimpse of gossamer
in the dashboard corner, my spider
patient predator even in the September chill
and on terms unfamiliar

tomorrow I'll set her free
though I fear the elements and fate
she is no local and the prairie wind cruel

if I set her in the branches of the tree
she might have one last meal
before her thread is cut

as I turn homeward
she, great architect of some grand design
I have not the wit to understand
spins on as though to prove
despite the odds and my incredulity
that the pattern is worth the effort

pilgrimage to Hardware Grill

~ for Russell

when we arrive
well-behaved reverent
clean-shaven and perfumed
we come to the temple
Russell of the brilliant smile
flatters me into my seat
charms you into yours
upon the linen-white altar
places our means to culinary salvation
the menu
the wine list

we peer and we purse our lips
an Ave for the appetizers
vespers for the veal
lobster sighs
porcine prayers
we take our time
we worshippers
we lovers three

Russell of the smile
materializes at your right hand
offers benediction
and a Californian Cabernet
we exhale and exalt
as he coaxes the cork
from the fine green neck
pours the nectar lovingly

we nod silent approval
our eyes shining humility
bending to our task
we break the bread

our voices low
past meals are reborn
remember the roast duckling
that brilliant Bordeaux
that first filet
that dessert divine and decadent
the timbre of our voices rises
as the colour to our cheeks
glasses to our lips
cheek to our tales
smiling Russell suavely
sets before us verdant greens
succulence swims in sauce
garrulous garlic wafts willfully
tastes scents textures
exotic exacting
our glasses
our hearts
are full
and we give thanks

salivating expectation
I roll my eyes
you your tongue across parted lips
we batten on ambrosia
our gentle mumbles
grow to groans gastronomique
crescendo to cries of capitulation
surrender to soft soft whimpers

forgive us
we know not what we do
now a fork
here a spoon
there a quaff
what can we not do
we happy three?

let us pilgrims three
Byron Shelley and Mary
go forth sail out
to Byzantium
Islands Virgin
Fields Elysian
we can write in the nude 'til noon
scribble skyclad under Orion
pen in the flesh at Aurora's call
each word a rite an offering
for the pagan feast at day's end

silently magically
our plates disappear
now we stare longingly
at the delectables
of our evening's final repast
selections made
we wander dreamily
back to forest glades
dance the bacchanal
we revellers three
Bacchus Dionysus Aphrodite

when beautiful saint Russell
offers final absolution
and I place the last morsel in my mouth
I know I love him
will always love him
we sip coffee and liqueurs
recall ecstasy in tranquility

our white linens are slightly soiled
but our souls cleansed
you burp discreetly
adjust your belt
I slip on my shoes
draw my hand through my hair
we leave our offering
tumble into the cool damp night
the glow of salvation alight in our faces

Tipscoggling

sometimes when stealing along back alleys
we stumble upon
treasures

alongside the gypsies
colourful and dirty-nailed
shy of a full set of teeth
tipscogglers of forgotten world lanes
we mine the wastebins of leftover tossed out lives

once we found
a huge bouquet of flowers
discarded like a bride's lost dream

another time
a huge ceramic flower pot
only one chip in its broad-grinning rim

once a wicker basket wanting only fruit
a magazine stand still eager for news
an antique bottle thirsting for life's elixir

re-discovered cycled newed

and last week
when no one was looking
not even the sun
we came across a bed of irises
purple heads anod
in a sea of weeds

and now their secret bulbs
are posited deep in the womb
of our own cunning flowerbeds

marking time

one two one two one two three
one two one two one two three
not bad this 7/8 life
bit of a risky rhythm
nothing I haven't danced before

one two one two one two three
one two one two one two three
reminds me that I still breathe
I'm still here and still raging
know more than I did yesterday

one two one two one two three
one two one two one two three
reminds me of the world's pace
furious hellbent caprice
one day at a tempest-tossed time

one two one two one two three
one two one two one two three
trying not to lose the beat
trying to make an honest
the madcap jazz combo plays on

one two one two one two three
one two one two one two three
these fools tripping mid-measure
and I seem lost among them
dancers caper dangerously

we're all marking time

Acknowledgements

My heartfelt gratitude goes out to

- my mother who inspired some of these poems, and who first taught me to read, to love words and music and stories.
- Duane Stewart who taught me poetry and Shakespeare and to delight in words.
- Thomas Trofimuk, fellow traveller on this road, wordsmith par excellence.
- my readers and listeners and hand-holders: Carolyn Pogue, Mark Haroun and Wally Diefenthaler.
- to my first editor-in-chief, Geoffrey Rowat McMaster (a.k.a. Otis, but don't get all big for your britches!).

Wintergreen Studios Press is an independent literary press. It is affiliated with the not-for-profit educational retreat centre, Wintergreen Studios, and supports the work of Wintergreen Studios by publishing works related to education, culture, and the environment.

www.wintergreenstudiospress.com
www.wintergreenstudios.com

18944442R00060

Made in the USA
Charleston, SC
28 April 2013